I0211054

# Serendipity in France

*poems by*

# Esther Sadoff

*Finishing Line Press*
Georgetown, Kentucky

# Serendipity in France

## ACKNOWLEDGMENTS

*Free State Review*: Serendipity and the mountain climber
*Jet Fuel Review*: Serendipity digs her feet in the sand
*South Florida Poetry Journal*: Serendipity and the two-piece




Publisher: Leah Huete de Maines
Editor: Christen Kincaid
Cover Art: Esther Sadoff
Author Photo: Esther Sadoff
Cover Design: Elizabeth Maines McCleavy and Esther Sadoff

Order online: www.finishinglinepress.com
                also available on amazon.com

Author inquiries and mail orders:
Finishing Line Press
PO Box 1626
Georgetown, Kentucky 40324
USA

# Contents

## Serendipity in France

Her voice is shrill above the din. The words come out thickly.
She orders a *pain au chocolat*, a coffee for here,
and a coffee to go then goes and sits,
nods, smiles (why is she always smiling?).
She pours two long packets of sugar,
sips her coffee, lifts the foam with a spoon.
She wants to see her face reflected somewhere.
She imagines her makeup drifting down her cheeks.
A pigeon is pecking breadcrumbs by her feet.
She feels the wind wafting as it takes off.
She savors words before she says them
but when she speaks she feels like she is holding
blocks in her mouth. Her lips can't fit around them
like when she got her braces off—her teeth felt slippery,
too big for weeks. Her lips were a curtain that wouldn't go down.
She feels words on the tip of her tongue,
words applauding on a crowded balcony
but the show hasn't begun.

## Serendipity's words feel like blocks

Serendipity's words feel like blocks jumbled
in her mouth, garbled sounds stuffed down her throat.
She wonders if her skin radiates worry.
Worry like commas scattered in a sentence.
She thinks she can withhold things, be *avare en mots*,
greedily gobbling her own thoughts before they can escape.
Maybe her body will stop shedding—hair, fingernail clippings.
She wants to clutch, save every piece of herself.
She thinks of the leafy shrub she cuts every year (or is it a weed?)—
bare branches turned bone-white, leaves falling like confetti.
When she speaks the words seem to fall everywhere too.
She confuses *partager* with *traverser*.
She means *Let's cross the street* but what comes out
is *Let's share* though there is nothing left to share.

## Serendipity bites her nails

There's a price for everything
and this is a cost that only she can pay.
So many people take from others
but Serendipity takes only from herself.
Sometimes she thinks about what her mind
is doing when she eats, moves, reads.
When she reads, the words aren't words
but a disembodied voice that tells her a story.
She wants to hold that voice,
to possess the thought that speaks to her arm,
the impulse that lifts food to her lips.
Sometimes her thoughts are like snakes.
She tries to follow them from tip to tongue.
She forgets so much that she wonders
if she will forget how to spell.
The letter u will be an upside down
umbrella collecting rain.
The letter v will be a finger tapping on a table.
On the bus, she sees a girl with a nose like a ski slope.
The girl's fingers are long and pink like flower petals.
On the train, Serendipity curls her fingers
into fists and tries to forget some more.

### Serendipity collects receipts

Each number is like a bird, a flock of tiny black slits.
She stuffs the crumpled rolls into her purse like tissue paper.
She searches for dates. She likes to remember
the different months, years, new and used clothes purchased.
She loves the tug and crack of a plastic tag snapping.
She loves to be reborn. Putting on a new dress
still makes her feel alive. One New Year's Eve,
she danced all night alone and didn't care.
She was radiating newness from a dress
she'd bought that afternoon. A pigeon-gray dress,
cinched and pleated at the waist. She folds the receipts,
takes pictures of herself in the long glass.
The pictures make her feel new as morning,
as the night sky freshly pierced with stars.

## Serendipity thought a coffee table

Serendipity thought a coffee table would make her whole
but her heart is a hole. She thinks about matching nightstands
with matching lamps like two umbrellas keeping away rain.
She wants everything to be clean like a desk at school,
wiped clean of pencil shavings and eraser crumbs.
She thinks having fun means fullness: a house full of clocks
and neatly folded socks. She wants her pictures framed.
She used to loiter on curbs, collecting flowerpots,
used hangers, a dented spinning chair.
Once, her house was full but she didn't know what to do with it all—
drawers with their handsome faces, their stolid handles.
When it rains the tables and chairs cast long shadows.
She wants to be the coffee table, but she is the tiny spoon
in the empty cup *stirring stirring stirring*.

## Serendipity blows with the wind

She wants to believe in reduction.
She wants to see how much she can subtract.
Can she be nothing but a verb? *Thinks, eats, sleeps.*
She loves to see how little she can say,
used to fantasize about saying so little that
all her words one day began to evaporate.
*One, two, three more birds* plucked from the sky.
She hopes her thoughts will stop taking shape,
like passengers on a disintegrating train.
Serendipity thinks about food.
*One, two, three bites* fewer.
It's almost like the food consumes
itself and then there's nothing left.

## Serendipity and the two-piece

She is at war with bathing suits.
She feels exposed in a one-piece.
Fear like a metal pole plunging through her chest.
She wonders if anyone can smell her fear.
She thinks that eyes have power so she looks away,
to the horizon softening from blue into white.
Serendipity is a student. She is studying what everything means.
Serendipity wants to be the blue umbrella unruffled by wind.
She fingers the crease at her brow, cemented from scowling.
She tries to straighten everything as if she were
a house full of crooked frames.
Serendipity's one-piece suit clings to her like a question,
but in a two-piece she feels the razor's edge,
two blades chopping her in half.

**Serendipity digs her feet in the sand**

She watches sand sift into each footprint like mini avalanches.
She wonders where the crabs go in winter.
Do they hide under all that sand? She tightens her hat on her head.
The water is marbled with prisms of drifting light.
She watches bodies crouch to flatten their towels.
Serendipity wonders if it's wrong to not want anything,
wonders what she should want, wonders how a hat stays on a head.
How a hat is someone's *volition*. Someone's desire to desire.
The bathing suit plunging at her neck is regret.
She feels exposed like ice melting into a puddle.
Like a pile of sand that used to be a castle.
It is crashing into the sea.

**Serendipity doesn't believe in advancement**

She believes in change. She believes in the ocean swallowing
rocks and fish.  When her parents speak about advancement,
she doesn't understand. She wonders what it would be like
to work in an office, the *click click click* of the mouse
like a slow and icy drip, the sound of chattering teeth.
But her chest is a canyon swarmed with bees.
Her mind is a mirror looking backwards.
Sometimes she catches a glimpse of herself.
Sometimes she sinks back into her skin, settles into her bones.
Sometimes she tingles with fear, with newness.
A long time ago she thought a road could take her anywhere.
When the lights rush past her window
fast enough she thinks she still can fly.

.

### Serendipity at the window

She watches the birds come and go toward the misty horizon.
Watches the profile of the sail boat as it turns, faraway angles
making it look so small. She watches the water froth,
a white bird flying into the sun. Today the clouds won't shift.
They hover like heavy pillows. The burnt rooftops are all orange glare.
Serendipity doesn't want to lie down. She sits at the ready,
she stands.  Ready to plunge, to dive into anything.
She is all nerves, a network of city lights. She's rehearsed her stance,
somewhere between drowning and waiting.
She pretends she is ironing a large sheet but it's really her heart.
She is pressing its creases flat. She is raising it like a white flag.

**Serendipity walks into the room**

Stands one foot in the room, one foot stepping
into the balcony, everyone turned away in conversation.
She feels the barrier between them.
Pretends to take an interest in a bird swooping nearby,
pretends to forget something, to remember something.
The strained moments are like tiny feet stepping all over her skin.
Who knew a room could be crowded with so many thoughts,
thoughts like rowboats paddling and knocking into each other?
She takes an interest in the ficus with its waxy leaves.
In the bougainvillea. She holds the word in her mouth.
*Bougainvillea.* She tells herself to never forget
what this flower looks like, to never forget its vibrancy
and volume, spilling over any balustrade or windowsill it meets.
She practices unlocking her tangled fingers,  tries to remember
any room can be an opening the further away you look.
Someone once said to talk to yourself like the child you were,
but she never could speak gently.
What if she were the sun to her own leaves?
What if she were the roots, the stem,
the fistfulls of tiny purple flowers?

### Serendipity and the two cups

She thought marriage would be like two cups on a table,
each poured into the other until they became even.
She believes in reason, tries to quiet her brain
but her brain is a forest that won't stop growing.
Growing up she loved to play with cups and water.
She'd balance and plunge the cups straight
to the bottom of the shallow pool,
then hold them still for as long as she could
before the air bubbles escaped and rose.
She imagined two worlds meeting—
pockets of air submerged in water
like passengers inside a submarine.
She told herself that her life depended
on holding those two cups steady.

**Serendipity looks away**

Serendipity is afraid of looking.
She used to be afraid of watching ice skaters skate.
Feared her eyes would distract, retract, didact.
She doesn't want to disrespect but she looks away
as if to hide her guilt. She tries to keep her gaze
on inanimate objects: *chair, table, cup.*
Anything that won't spook or startle.
In conversation, she wonders about the machinery of speech,
what keeps a person talking, blinking, thinking.
She thinks about counting her blinks but defects,
circles back to the mouth, the lips forming words.
Maybe a thing can't break if you don't watch it fall.
By the time she reclaims her gaze (sugars, stirs, sips),
the ice-skater spins, lands, dips, drops to a bow.
Sweet crystals sugar the table's surface like flecks of ice.

## Serendipity is finite

She has learned to hate the cruise ships stacked
like seven-decker cakes towering over city streets.
For days the sky has been confused with water—
gray particles dusting the landscape, fogging the mountains.
She confuses the sound of seagulls with the cries of children.
The other day she saw a rat running down a telephone pole.
She heard cats meowing in sewer drains.
Serendipity feels her body turning, sometimes tumbling
like clothes in a washer machine.
All her dirty clothes are lying against a wall.
She hasn't felt alone in so long but she feels aloneness
waiting for her like fingernails tapping against a wall.
Aloneness like ordering bread at the bakery
but every day it comes back burnt.
Aloneness like the branch of the thorn bush she ran into yesterday
when running in the dark. It scraped her face and arms.
She cried out but no one heard.

**Serendipity tells a story**

She wants to believe in a beginning, middle, and end,
but she is a thousand beginnings like a thousand
cups pulled each day from the cabinet.
She watches the clouds blur into the sky.
She watches the coffee make dark rings in her cup.
She opens her drawers, takes things out, and puts them away.
Sometimes fear spiders itself back into her heart.
Fear feels like an ice pick, a mountaineer breaking down the ice.
But here she is hot and always burning.
Her feet are steaming, smoking
like the restaurants coming alive at night.
Serendipity was never very good at telling a story.
She needs a viewer to help it take shape.
She needs to see herself through someone else's eyes.
Growing up she could never see herself clearly.
Could only see herself by comparison: *Skinnier than. Bigger than.*
She was always waiting for someone else to tell her.
At night she reads books and looks for signs.
She misreads *resemble* for *reassemble*. Confuses *acre* for *make her.*

## Serendipity and the submersible

The submersible has gone missing.
Somehow five people were crowded into a metal bean
and dunked into the sea two miles deep.
Rescuers hear banging at the site where contact was lost,
banging like a fist inside a box.
Serendipity has heard the sound of outer space,
the roar and clang of black holes though she knows
those sounds wouldn't be sounds without ears to hear.
She thinks she knows something of suffocation,
has been giving her oxygen to others for years.
She has tried to control the weather, to keep others safe,
would blame herself for snow and sleet.
She and her husband have avoided elevators for years,
have taken to stairwells, have practiced not caring.
Not caring meaning *forgetting*. But the world is infinite.
One day, they decide to step into a narrow elevator.
The floor numbers are graffitied with pens and scraped with keys.
When it stalls once, twice, and the door won't open,
their eyes meet and she wonders if bad luck is real.
Serendipity thinks about the submersible and its tiny controller.
She tries to invent new ways to breathe.

**Serendipity is a good student**

In a new city, she takes pictures of street corners.
She lays down tracks to follow back.
She retraces her step, reads, and rereads
and eventually gets home.
She names each morning after a color
(yellow, orange, pink, and purple)
like cataloging papers into folders.
Here the afternoons are all blue.
An endless robin egg sky that won't break.
A baby bird that just won't hatch.
She fills her bag, packing for every contingency.
You can't make a mistake if you fold everything
inside of you, the way she used to fold herself
under her blanket—fearing the Moon would find her
and tell Night to turn her into stars.
Stars blown like grains of sand across the sky.
On the beach she looks inward. Then downward.
Outlines her legs with seashells and stones.
She doesn't know if a place can change her,
rearrange her like the shifting sands—
yellow, orange, blue, purple. One of each color
to outline her knees, her browning thighs, the stacks
of books around the house to outline her mind.

### Serendipity and the mountain climber

She wakes and feels the ice pick in her chest.
The mountain climber is hacking away at her again.
She feels the ice pick jam into her heart, feels the shards
of ice slip and scatter into the expanse below.
The mountain climber believes in speed.
She is cold all over. She feels alone
like a paper bag blown high into a tree.
Alone like a whale 2000 feet deep in the sea.
Breathing feels secondary.  She forgets she has
a mouth and nose, aware only of eyes that open and close.
When she coughs, the mountain climber is rattled.
Coughing gives sudden shape and breadth to her lungs.
The mountain climber hangs on with one hand,
the ice pick glints sharp and loose in the other.

**Serendipity is obsessed with straws**

At school they learned that if you smoked,
you'd soon breathe like you were breathing through a straw.
On Mount Everest the straw would shrink as thin as a needle.
In wellness class, they breathed through straws,
wore drunk goggles, and watched the world warp and spin.
After school, she snapped all her mother's cigarettes in half,
put pictures of charred lungs on the refrigerator.
Sometimes she dribbled water into the white carton.
The doctor told Serendipity that if she ever smoked,
she would have an asthma attack and suffocate,
head dizzily spinning over new soccer cleats.
Running up the stairs, she thinks of the straw siphoning off
all vitality until she heaves. She pinches her nose to see how
little she can breathe, how much she can withstand.
She wants to pluck the mountaineer from
the mountain's peak, let fly an inrush of wind.

## Serendipity dreams

Each time her voice is louder. She has been swallowing all sound,
but she continues to dial, a collect call to *herself* but she's never home.
She lets it go to the last ring, watches her skin brown,
pale skin still hidden within the creases of her roughened hands.
She thinks her hands are not her hands. Takes two, three steps back.
She needs distance to know what she lacks.
She sees a huge building all in yellow with wide windows by the sea.
Inside, there's a gallery full of paintings—hundreds of them
stacked against a wall but her own painting is gone.
When she wakes, she shivers away the strangeness
like a dog shaking away rain. For a few moments her body is hers—
she is in the yellow room; the painting on the wall bears her signature.
When the phone rings, she recreates her voice, her mouth.
She breathes herself into herself repeats *hello hello hello* always louder.

## Serendipity at the gift shop

She buys perfectly browned squares of canistrelli
flavored with lemon, anise, and almonds.
She takes few pictures, keeps her lips sealed
until it's customary, necessary to speak.
She knows just how to speak so that her throat becomes a bridge.
A bridge with water rising under it.
At night the water swells into a river.
She stops to flip through magazines,
fingers the flower-bright covers.
Flipping from page to page feels like surgery on her brain.
Leaving the gift shop, she balances the bags against her chest.
She always refuses a bag to carry her things.
Whatever she takes with her she wants to hold.
She mistakes gratitude for taking the shape of what you own.

## Serendipity and the balcony

She can hear the next-door neighbor vacuuming in the morning,
the woman watering the plants lethargically with the heavy hose.
Now a broom brushing against the wooden slats.
She sees a shirtless man looking through a drying rack.
The mourning dove arrives each day
and marches up and down the balcony.
She feels the lean of each building. She feels like she could fall.
Each day she travels forward. When she was little, she would play
with colorful rings in the swimming pool. She didn't want to swim
but couldn't stop tossing them, forced to dive to retrieve
the orange, red, blue, and green hoops. She kept diving and diving.
She learned to love the plunge, the unearthliness, the upside-down.
In the ocean, she tightens her mask and dives. She grazes her fingers
over the sandy rills. There are fish translucent as light.
She keeps pressing her fingers between those ridges.
She tries not to disrupt, to disturb.
Still believes she can touch without taking.

**Serendipity looks for lucky spiral shells in the surf**

According to legend, Lucy tore out her eyes
 and threw them into the sea.
Ever since, her eyes have proliferated—
creamy white spirals that wash up on the beach.
Serendipity sees one in the rubble,
ruddy backing catching the light.
She clutches it between her toes,
holds it back from the surge,
finds another one chipped
and faded as an old button.
On the way back she needs
her hands free as she climbs over jagged rocks.
She tucks the broken shell in her suit,
cradles the perfectly round shell in her mouth—
delicate as a hinge, a dollop of cream.
She wants to hold something without fear
of swallowing, of becoming. Just the risk of belief—
the chance to hold luck between her teeth.

**Serendipity wonders what happens to a body**

In the comments section, someone asks what happens to a body
12,000 feet deep in the sea and Serendipity can't help but look.
One commenter says the human body is incinerated.
One says it turns into slime that shivers at the bottom of the sea.
She too is afraid of darkness, runs down the hallway
when all the lights are off to avoid the unknown.
She can't stop thinking of the highest and lowest places—
a mountain climber above the clouds; a nineteen-year-old
in the *Titan*, nose nervously pressed to the glass.
The body is rediscovered every day—knees creaking
as she rises from the bed, arms strengthened
so she can lift anything over her head.
She's always wedged between two tenses,
hedged between two directions. She wants to hold
without having, to place without possessing.
She still wonders if a body is worth having.

**Serendipity has no speech**

When she speaks, she has meaning
but she never says what she means.
The meaning hangs in her head like an ornament.
A voice can erase itself. She buys a bracelet with turquoise beads.
She thinks a bead can hold something, invoke something.
She thinks she can catch something, give shape to hope or pain.
She convinces herself to believe in magic
as if she could trick her own brain.
Sometimes Google suggests what she really means,
gives rise to desire, gives her questions shape and character.
On the airplane home she promises to remember
the jolt of a speeding car, the humid sea air,
the strain and burn of walking up hill after hill.
She still dreams of trading places with anything: *rock, leaf, or ledge*.
Still dreams of a place that won't let her go.

**Esther Sadoff** is a teacher and writer from Columbus, Ohio. Her poems have been featured or are forthcoming in *Up the Staircase Quarterly, Hole in the Head Review, Little Patuxent Review, Jet Fuel Review, Cathexis Poetry Northwest, Pidgeonholes, Red Ogre Review, South Florida Poetry Journal,* among others. She is the author of several chapbooks: *Some Wild Woman*, Finishing Line Press; *Dear Silence,* Kelsay Books; and *If I Hold My Breath*, Bottlecap Press. She was nominated for a Pushcart in 2023 by Hole in the Head Review.

www.ingramcontent.com/pod-product-compliance
Lightning Source LLC
Chambersburg PA
CBHW022102080426
42734CB00009B/1464